TRAVERSE
THEATRE

TRAVERSE THEATRE COMPANY

FAMILY
3 plays
ACTS by Riccardo Galgani
director Yvonne McDevitt

Marie	Una McLean
Jack	Russell Hunter
Pat	Liam Brennan

ONE GOOD BEATING by Linda McLean
director Philip Howard

Robert	Russell Hunter
Stephen	Liam Brennan
Elaine	Jennifer Black

THE VISITOR by Iain Crichton Smith
director Philip Howard

Helen	Una McLean
George	Russell Hunter
Heine	Liam Brennan

designer	Neil Warmington
lighting designer	Chris Davey
composer	John Harris
voice coach	Ros Steen
stage manager	Victoria Paulo
deputy stage manager	Jess Richards
assistant stage manager	Mikey Graham
wardrobe supervisor	Lynn Ferguson
wardrobe assistant	Alice Taylor

First performed at the Traverse Theatre Friday 5 February 1999.

TRAVERSE THEATRE

One of the most important theatres in Britain The Observer

Edinburgh's **Traverse Theatre** is Scotland's new writing theatre, with a 36 year record of excellence. With quality, award-winning productions and programming, the Traverse receives accolades at home and abroad from audiences and critics alike.

The Traverse has an unrivalled reputation for producing contemporary theatre of the highest quality, invention and energy, commissioning and supporting writers from Scotland and around the world and facilitating numerous script development workshops, rehearsed readings and public writing workshops. The Traverse aims to produce several major new theatre productions plus a Scottish touring production each year. It is unique in Scotland in its exclusive dedication to new writing, providing the infrastructure, professional support and expertise to ensure the development of a sustainable and relevant theatre culture for Scotland and the UK.

Traverse Theatre Company productions have been seen worldwide including in London, Toronto, Budapest and New York. Recent touring successes in Scotland include PERFECT DAYS by Liz Lochhead (January-March '99), PASSING PLACES by Stephen Greenhorn, HERITAGE by Nicola McCartney and LAZYBED by Iain Crichton Smith.

The Traverse can be relied upon to produce more good-quality new plays than any other Fringe venue
Daily Telegraph

During the Edinburgh Festival the Traverse is one of the most important venues with world class premieres playing daily in the two theatre spaces. The Traverse won *ten* awards at the 1998 Edinburgh Festival Fringe, including *Scotsman Fringe Firsts* for Traverse productions KILL THE OLD TORTURE THEIR YOUNG by David Harrower and PERFECT DAYS by Liz Lochhead.

An essential element of the Traverse Company's activities takes place within the educational sector, concentrating on the process of playwriting for young people. The Traverse flagship education project BANK OF SCOTLAND CLASS ACT offers young people in schools the opportunity to work with theatre professionals and see their work performed on the Traverse stage. In addition the Traverse Young Writers group, led by professional playwrights, has been running for almost three years and meets weekly.

THE WRITERS

Riccardo Galgani lives and works in Glasgow. He has written, directed and produced two short films and is currently working on several projects including a PhD in Philosophy from the University of Sussex, a feature film called *Galloway* and a new full-length play.

ACTS is Riccardo's first play.

Linda McLean's work for the theatre includes *The Price of a Good Dinner* (Derby Playhouse); co-author of *The Corridor* (Benchtours). Work for radio includes *Take One Egg* for Radio 4. She is under commission to the Traverse and Paines Plough and is currently writing a play for Radio 4.

ONE GOOD BEATING was first presented as a workshop production at the Traverse during *Naked Stages*.

Iain Crichton Smith (1928 - 1998) was one of Scotland's most important literary figures this century. Born in Glasgow and brought up on the Isle of Lewis, he taught English in schools from 1955 to 1977, after which he became a full-time writer of poems, novels, short stories and plays in both English and Gaelic.

Iain's published works include the novels *Consider the Lilies*, *The Last Summer*, *In The Middle of the Wood* and *An Honourable Death*. The Traverse Theatre Company produced his play *Lazybed* in 1997. His many honours include an OBE and Honorary Doctorates from the Universities of Dundee, Glasgow and Aberdeen as well as many awards, including four Book Society Awards and the Commonwealth Poetry prize.

THE VISITOR, loosely adapted from his own short story, was commissioned by the Traverse and is Iain Crichton Smith's last work.

FOREWORD

The three plays which make up this FAMILY are of course thematically linked, but those links are there to be discovered by audience or reader, and are less important than the spirit or *genius* of each play: each was written without knowledge of one another. It may not be remarkable then that three very different playwrights should be coinciding around the hearth of the universal institution, but what unites the writing is the precision with which they dissect it, whether it be the return of the prodigal son, the father/daughter bond, or even the family riven by an outside force.

Commentators from outside Scotland tend to assume that a Scottish play isn't so Scottish unless it is fiercely political; not only is this analysis a decade out of date, it also misunderstands the point at which the personal ends and the political begins. Scottish playwrights have a proud tradition of examining both at the same time with the mercilessness of a vivisectionist.

And if three playwrights choose the FAMILY as their setting, it may just be a sign of cultural confidence that Scottish writers, who have made a significant contribution to the drive for political and constitutional change, can set their targets so unapologetically on the domestic.

Philip Howard
Traverse Theatre
February 1999

BIOGRAPHIES
in alphabetical order

JENNIFER BLACK (*Elaine*): Trained: RSAMD. For the Traverse: KILL THE OLD TORTURE THEIR YOUNG, THE BENCH, HOUSE AMONG THE STARS. Other theatre work includes: THE TRICK IS TO KEEP BREATHING (Tron/Toronto/Royal Court); GOOD, THE BABY, LAVOCHKIN 5 (Tron); BURIED TREASURE (Bush); ASHES TO ASHES (Ghostown); CARMEN: THE PLAY, SACRED HEARTS (Communicado); DEAD FUNNY, ON GOLDEN POND, BLITHE SPIRIT, TRIVIAL PURSUITS (Royal Lyceum). Television work includes: THE BILL (Thames); TAGGART (STV); HI-DE-HI (BBC). Film work includes: LOCAL HERO, HEAVENLY PURSUITS. Radio work includes: WEEK-ENDING; THE TRICK IS TO KEEP BREATHING.

LIAM BRENNAN (*Pat, Stephen, Heine*): For the Traverse: KNIVES IN HENS (festival 97), WORMWOOD. Other theatre work includes seasons and productions with Dundee Rep, Perth Rep, Royal Lyceum, Sheffield Crucible, Borderline, Cumbernauld Theatre, Salisbury Playhouse, Brunton Theatre, Durham Theatre Company and Calypso Productions, Dublin. Recent theatre includes: *Macbeth* in MACBETH (Brunton); *Edmund* in KING LEAR, MERCHANT OF VENICE (Sheffield Crucible); *Michael Collins* in GOD SAVE IRELAND CRIED THE HERO (Wiseguise); BABYCAKES (Clyde Unity). TV includes: TAGGART, STRATHBLAIR II, HIGH ROAD, MACHAIR. Radio includes numerous plays and short stories for the BBC.

CHRIS DAVEY (lighting designer): For the Traverse: PASSING PLACES, GRETA. Theatre work includes: THE DEEP BLUE SEA, CLAY BULL (Royal Lyceum); ANNA KARENINA, JANE EYRE, THE MILL ON THE FLOSS, DESIRE UNDER THE ELMS (Shared Experience); BROTHERS OF THE BRUSH, HAPPY VALLEY (Everyman, Liverpool); THE ILLUSION (Royal Exchange, Manchester); THEN AGAIN (Lyric, Hammersmith); TROILUS AND CRESSIDA, A MONTH IN THE COUNTRY, EVERYMAN, THE COMEDY OF ERRORS, EASTER (Royal Shakespeare Company); WAR AND PEACE (Royal National Theatre & Shared Experience). Opera work includes: THE PICTURE OF DORIAN GRAY (Opera de Monte Carlo); SCHUMANN SONG CYCLES (Batignano Opera, Tuscany).

JOHN HARRIS (composer) For the Traverse: PERFECT DAYS (on tour & festival 98), ANNA WEISS, KNIVES IN HENS, GRETA, SHARP SHORTS. Other theatre work includes: IL BELLISSIMO SILENCIO, STOCKAREE, OF NETTLES AND ROSES (Theatre Workshop); NOT FOR THE FANFARE (First Base); THE NEST, M'LADY MALADE, THE GREAT THEATRE OF THE WORLD, MANKIND, THE TEMPEST (True Belleek). Musical Direction includes: MASS (Bernstein); AFRICAN SANCTUS (Fanshawe); CARMINA BURANA (Orff); HIAWATHA (Bogdanov). John is also commissioned as a classical composer and works as assistant organist at St Giles' Cathedral, Edinburgh.

PHILIP HOWARD (director): Trained: Royal Court Theatre on the Regional Theatre Young Director Scheme, 1988-90. Associate Director at the Traverse 1993-6, and Artistic Director since1996. Productions at the Traverse include: LOOSE ENDS, BROTHERS OF THUNDER, EUROPE, KNIVES IN HENS (also Bush Theatre), THE ARCHITECT, FAITH HEALER, WORMWOOD, LAZYBED, THE CHIC NERDS, KILL THE OLD TORTURE THEIR YOUNG and HERITAGE. Other theatre includes HIPPOLYTUS (Arts,Cambridge); ENTERTAINING MR SLOANE (Royal, Northampton); SOMETHING ABOUT US (Lyric Hammersmith Studio).

RUSSELL HUNTER (*Jack, Robert, George*): Now in his 53rd year in the theatre. Recent appearances at the Traverse: David Harrower's KILL THE OLD TORTURE THEIR YOUNG (festival '98) and James Duthie's GRETA (December '97). Most recent theatre work: *Chetbutykin* in Chekov's THREE SISTERS (Birmingham Rep).

YVONNE MCDEVITT (director): Trained: Trinity College, Dublin. Assistant directing work includes: THE INVISIBLE WOMAN (Gate); MISS JULIE (Lyric Hammersmith). Directing work includes: NOT I, ROCKABY (Dublin Theatre Festival and Moscow); THE LOTTERY TICKET (The Red Room); GENES (October Gallery). Yvonne is currently training at the Traverse on the Regional Theatre Young Director Scheme and has assisted on PERFECT DAYS and KILL THE OLD TORTURE THEIR YOUNG as well as working on COLOURS OF THE CHAMELEON.

UNA MCLEAN (*Marie, Helen*): For the Traverse: THE ARCHITECT, SKY WOMAN FALLING, INES DE CASTRO, BLENDING IN. Other theatre work includes: WOMAN IN MIND, ARSENIC & OLD LACE, MRS WARREN'S PROFESSION, A PASSIONATE WOMAN (Pitlochry Festival Theatre). In 1998 Una played *Albertine* at 70 in a tour of Michel Tremblay's ALBERTINE IN FIVE TIMES (Clyde Unity) and was in the original production of THE GUID SISITERS (Tron). Film includes: THE DEBT COLLECTOR by Anthony Neilson, soon to be released.

NEIL WARMINGTON (designer): Graduated in Fine Art at Maidstone College of Art before attending the post-graduate theatre design course at Motley. For the Traverse: PASSING PLACES (TMA Award Best Design). Recent theatre credits include: THE DUCHESS OF MALFI (Bath); JANE EYRE (Shared Experience/Young Vic); WOMEN LAUGHING (Watford); THE TEMPEST (Contact, Manchester); DESIRE UNDER THE ELMS (Shared Experience); DISSENT, ANGELS IN AMERICA (7:84 Scotland); TROILUS AND CRESSIDA (Opera North); HENRY V (Royal Shakespeare Company); MUCH ADO ABOUT NOTHING (Queen's Theatre, Shaftesbury Ave); THE LIFE OF STUFF (Donmar Warehouse); LIFE IS A DREAM (TMA Award Best Design), FIDDLER ON THE ROOF (West Yorkshire Playhouse); WAITING FOR GODOT, MUCH ADO ABOUT NOTHING (Liverpool Everyman); THE GLASS MENAGERIE, COMEDIANS, MERLIN (Parts 1& 2) (Royal Lyceum); BLITHE SPIRIT (York Theatre Royal); I PUT A SPELL ON YOU (Leicester Haymarket); CORIOLANUS (Tramway); CRAZYHORSE (Paines Plough); OEDIPUS REX (Connecticut State Opera); TAMING OF THE SHREW (English Touring Theatre). Neil designed the launch of Glasgow's Year of Architecture 1999. He has also won The Linbury Prize for stage design and The Sir Alfred Munnings Florence prize for painting.

FAMILY

sets, props & costumes created by Traverse workshops
funded by the National Lottery

Traverse computer systems funded by the National Lottery

for FAMILY:

scenic artist Ursula Cleary

production photography Kevin Low

print photography Euan Myles

wardrobe care LEVER BROTHERS

TRAVERSE THEATRE • THE COMPANY

SPONSORSHIP

Sponsorship income enables the Traverse to commission and produce new plays and offer audiences a diverse and exciting programme of events throughout the year.

We would like to thank the following companies for their support throughout the year.

✻ BANK OF SCOTLAND

ESPC

4 Basilica
COMPUTING LTD
WWW.BASILICA.CO.UK

CORPORATE ASSOCIATE SCHEME
LEVEL ONE
Balfour Beatty
Scottish Life the PENSION company
United Distillers & Vintners

LEVEL TWO
Laurence Smith -
Wine Merchants
NB Information
Willis Corroon Scotland Ltd

LEVEL THREE
Alistir Tait FGA -
Antiques & Fine Jewellery
Allingham & Co, Solicitors
Nicholas Groves Raines -
Architects
McCabe Partnership -
Chartered Accountants
KPMG
Scottish Post Office Board

With thanks to
Navy Blue Design, print designers for the Traverse and to George Stewarts the printers.
Purchase of the Traverse Box Office and computer network has been made possible with funds from the National Lottery.

The Traverse Theatre's work would not be possible without the support of

THE SCOTTISH ARTS COUNCIL   · EDINBVRGH ·
THE CITY OF EDINBURGH COUNCIL

The Traverse receives financial assistance for its educational and development work from
John Lewis Partnership, Save and Prosper Charitable Trusts, Binks Trust, The Bulldog Prinsep Theatrical Fund, Calouste Gulbenkian Foundation
The Traverse has the support of The Mackintosh Foundation under the Regional Theatre Young Director Scheme administrated by Channel Four Television. Charity No. SC002368

ACTS

Riccardo Galgani

Characters

MARIE

JACK

PAT

Setting: a flat in Glasgow.

Act One

MARIE, *an old woman in her eighties, sits on a chair by a table in the kitchen. She sits on the left of the table, facing the stage. There is another chair on the right and a stool in the middle. She looks out the window frame to her right. Throughout she fluctuates from lucidity to distraction, to regression, to a catatonic state.*

MARIE. Yiv burn't it.

Pause.

MARIE. Yiv burn't the toast.

JACK. Wha' are yi sayin'?

MARIE. I said yiv burn't the toast.

JACK, *an old man in his eighties, enters.*

JACK. Can yi no watch it yersel?

MARIE. Yi know fine well I can't.

JACK. Gie it a scrape.

MARIE. I'm no eatin' burn't toast.

JACK. Scrape off the burn't bits.

MARIE. I'll have a fresh slice.

JACK. You'll eat what's there.

MARIE. I'm no eatin' that.

JACK. T' heng wi yi.

Silence. MARIE *takes a bite of the toast.*

MARIE. I'm no eatin' the crust.

JACK. Nobodies askin' yi t' eat the crust.

MARIE. Aye, well, I'm no eatin' it anyway.

Silence.

MARIE. Aye, a wee dog would be nice.

JACK. What are yi sayin now?

MARIE. I said a wee dog would be nice.

JACK. What would yi want a wee dog fir?

MARIE. A wee something t' pet.

JACK. Aye, an pass yer crusts to.

He picks up the paper.

MARIE. What kind o' day is it?

JACK. What kind o' day?

MARIE. Aye, what kind o' day?

JACK. What? Are yi thinking o' going out?

Pause.

MARIE. No. That tree's looking a wee bit bare.

JACK. Aye, well it would.

MARIE. Them leaves are having a time of it, trying to hold on in the wind.

JACK. Aye.

MARIE. Was it windy when yi went out for yer paper?

JACK. Aye, it was.

MARIE. Makes yer eyes stream.

Pause.

MARIE. Who's that man there? He should be away at work in Edinburgh the day.

Pause.

JACK. Put the radio on.

MARIE. What do you want the radio on for?

JACK. It's something to listen to at least.

MARIE. You've got your paper.

JACK. Aye, I've got my paper.

Silence for a few minutes. MARIE*'s head falls forward and she sleeps for a few moments. The doorbell rings.*

MARIE. Who will that be?

JACK. How the heng would I know.

MARIE. It'll be the cleaner.

JACK. It'll no be the cleaner.

The bell rings again and JACK *gets up.*

MARIE. Jack, who is it?

Pause.

MARIE. Jack?

Into the kitchen walks a man in his early fifties.

PAT. Mum.

MARIE. Who's that?

PAT. It's me.

MARIE. Me?

PAT. Yes, me.

MARIE. Who?

PAT. Pat.

MARIE. Pat?

PAT. Aye, Pat.

MARIE. Is that my Pat?

PAT. Aye, it is.

MARIE. Pat, O, I never thought I'd see yi again. Come here so's I can see yi an' give yi a kiss. Let me see how well yi are. Oh, Pat.

PAT *sits next to* MARIE, *on the stool, with his back facing the audience. Whenever he gets up and moves about he always returns to this position.* MARIE *looks at him for a while and then drifts off again, staring vacantly into space and out the window. He sits there and looks at her.* JACK *has not yet come back into the room and* PAT *keeps looking at the door.*

PAT. How are yi then Mum?

MARIE. O, I'm fine.

PAT. Fine.

MARIE. Aye.

PAT. That's good.

MARIE. Apart from mi eyes.

PAT. What's wrong with yer eyes?

MARIE Och, I can't see out o' this one at all an' this one only works every now and then.

PAT. Are yer glasses no good?

MARIE. Aye, me glasses.

JACK *comes back into the room.* PAT *stands up.* JACK *sits down.* PAT, *after a pause, sits back down.*

PAT. Mum says her eyes are bad.

JACK. There's nothing wrong wi her eyes.

PAT. What about yersel?

JACK. Aye.

PAT. You're well?

JACK. I'm aright.

PAT. Good.

JACK. Apart from ma knee.

PAT. Yir knee?

JACK. Aye.

PAT. What's wrong with yer knee?

JACK. I can't walk on it too well.

PAT. That's a shame.

JACK. Aye. It is.

PAT. I know how much yi like yer walks.

JACK. I do.

PAT. I know.

JACK. But not so much now.

PAT. No.

JACK. No.

PAT. D'yi not get out much then?

JACK. Och, out t' get the papers.

MARIE. That's not the only place he goes.

JACK. What would you know?

MARIE. How many d'you know that take an hour t' get the papers an' come back smellin' o' whiskey an' fallin asleep on the chair for the rest of the day.

PAT. Is that what you do Dad?

MARIE. Is that what he does? I'm just after tellin' yi that that's what he does.

Pause.

MARIE. Make the boy a cup o' tea Jack. D'yi want a cup o' tea?

PAT. No thanks.

MARIE. No?

PAT. I don't drink tea.

MARIE. What d'yi mean yi don't drink tea.

PAT. I don't drink it.

MARIE. Everyone drinks tea.

PAT. I don't like it.

MARIE. Yi never used t' not like it.

PAT. I've never liked it.

MARIE. Jack, will yi not put the kettle on an' make the lad a cup o' tea.

PAT. Dad, sit down.

JACK *gets up and puts the kettle on.*

JACK. How many sugar's d' yi take?

PAT. None.

MARIE. No sugar?

PAT. No.

MARIE. What about that? Jack, what are yi doin' with that mug?

JACK. What d' yi think I'm doin' with it?

MARIE. Get one o' the nice one's out of the sideboard.

JACK. This one will do fine.

MARIE. That's a fine way t' treat a guest. Gie him a mangy auld mug.

JACK. There's nothing wrong wi' the mug.

MARIE. No for you there's no. Shall I get up an' get them masel?

JACK. Och, stay where yi are.

JACK *leaves.*

MARIE. Aye. D' yi still like a wee biscuit wi yer tea?

PAT. You haven't finished your breakfast.

MARIE. Yi were always fond o' yer biscuits. Don't forget t' feed yersel.

PAT. I won't.

MARIE. It soon tells if yi don't.

PAT. What about you?

MARIE. I never think o' masel, it's always only other's I feel for.

JACK *returns.*

MARIE. Why have yi brought in three?

JACK. Are yi no having tea yersel?

MARIE. Aye, but I don't need a china tea cup t' drink it out of. Use the mugs, you in all.

JACK. T' heng wi' yi.

MARIE. See the way he talks t' me. What a way. Jack, gie it a rinse first.

PAT. Dad, sit down.

MARIE. He'll sit down when he's made the tea.

JACK *sits down whilst the kettle boils.*

MARIE. Yir looking a wee bit thin.

PAT. I'm no.

MARIE. Yi are. Would yi no say he's looking a wee bit thin?

JACK. He looks the same as before.

MARIE. Before?

JACK. Aye.

MARIE. How long's that then?

JACK. Twelve years.

MARIE. Twelve years?

JACK. Aye.

MARIE. Yiv no been t' see yer mother for twelve years.

PAT. No.

JACK. Aye.

MARIE. How old would I 'ave been then?

JACK. Seventy-two.

MARIE. Seventy-two. How old am I now then?

JACK. Eighty-four.

MARIE. A well.

JACK. Aye.

MARIE. Have I changed much?

PAT. Not at all.

MARIE. Have I no?

PAT. No.

MARIE. That's good.

Silence.

PAT. I brought yi a wee present.

MARIE. A present.

PAT. Aye.

MARIE. That's nice.

PAT. Here.

MARIE. Jack.

She hands the wrapped gift to JACK.

MARIE. Open that, it's from Pat. Yi shouldn't waste yer money on presents.

PAT. I wanted to get you something.

MARIE. Ah well, that's nice o' you. What is it Jack?

JACK. A frame.

MARIE. A frame?

JACK. Aye, a frame.

Hands it to her.

MARIE. What's in the frame?

JACK. It's a new frame.

MARIE. Is that yer wife an' boys?

PAT. No.

MARIE. That's lovely.

PAT. It's no ma wife an' boys.

MARIE. Who is it then?

PAT. It's nobody.

MARIE. Nobody. Sure it's not nobody. It's a fine looking
family. Sure, that's you there.

PAT. No, it's not, it's the picture they put in with the frame.
It's nobody.

MARIE. Not yer wife.

PAT. No.

MARIE. That's a shame. A lovely looking woman. O, aye,
I see now.

PAT. You see.

MARIE. Aye. Jack, put that on the mantelpiece.

    JACK *takes the frame and leaves the room. Silence.*

PAT. The flat's looking nice and clean.

MARIE. Aye, a wee woman comes round.

PAT. Does she?

MARIE. Aye.

PAT. That's good. Is she nice?

MARIE. She's no very good at the cleanin'.

PAT. Is she no.

MARIE. No. Yer Dad has t' go round after her wi a brush.

PAT. You should get someone else.

MARIE. Can yi pass me that jar?

PAT. This one?

MARIE. No, the brown one.

PAT. For yer eyes.

MARIE. Mi eyes. No. There's nothing they can do for mi eyes.

PAT. What are they for then?

MARIE. Ma kidneys.

PAT. Yer kidneys.

MARIE. Aye.

PAT. What's wrong wi them?

MARIE. O, son, if I was t' tell yi what's wrong wi ma kidneys an' liver an' heart an bones. I'm as stiff as a table.

PAT. You're not.

MARIE. I've no got long left.

PAT. Yi have.

MARIE. No, I haven't.

PAT. Yi spend all yer life thinking yer dying.

MARIE. Aye, well, I'm ready t' leave the world. I hope I'm ready t' leave the world.

PAT. Don't say that.

MARIE. All so far away.

Pause.

It's nice o' yi t' come an' see yer mother before she goes.

PAT. I wanted t' see yi.

MARIE. That's a good boy. I thought I'd never see yi again.

PAT. I'm here now.

MARIE. So yi are.

PAT. I am.

MARIE. Out of the blue. Yer mother's soul was almost away. An' yir glad t' see me?

PAT. It's lovely t' see yi.

MARIE. That's nice. Now, be good t' yersel son, no-one else will.

JACK *comes back in.*

MARIE. Twelve years. Is that what yi said Jack?

JACK. Aye.

MARIE. How long's that then?

JACK. Twelve years.

MARIE. Aye. How old was I then?

JACK. Seventy-two.

MARIE. Seventy-two. Was I?

JACK. Aye.

MARIE. Jack, have yi not made that boy a cup o' tea.

PAT. Dad, I'm alright.

JACK. I'll get yi his tea.

JACK *gets back up and pours the kettle.*

MARIE. Is that water boiling?

JACK. Aye it's boiling.

MARIE. Scalding?

JACK. Aye.

MARIE. Gie the lad some biscuits as well.

JACK *goes into the cupboard and takes out some biscuits and hands them to* PAT.

MARIE. Is that how we serve tea. What about a wee plate for the biscuits?

PAT. This is fine.

MARIE. Put them on a plate Jack.

JACK. There yi are.

He then hands him the tea.

MARIE. That'll warm yi up.

PAT. Thanks.

MARIE. Can yi no make a cup o' tea.

JACK. Aye.

MARIE. There's no milk.

JACK. There's none in here.

MARIE. He can't have a cup o' tea wi'out any milk.

PAT. It's okay.

MARIE. Jack.

JACK is already out of the room.

Act Two

As before.

PAT. He still likes his walks then.

MARIE. Aye.

PAT. Does he go far?

MARIE. As far as the pub. Di yi no want some milk in yer tea?

PAT. There isn't any milk.

MARIE. Take plenty o milk in yer tea.

PAT. That's where Dad's gone.

MARIE. Where?

PAT. To get some milk.

MARIE. Has he?

PAT. Yes.

MARIE. That's good. Yi need yer milk.

MARIE*'s head drops forwards. Sleeps for a few seconds, wakes.*

MARIE. Get out of my sight.

PAT. It's me.

MARIE. I know fine well it's you, get out of my sight.

PAT. Pat.

MARIE. Pat, oh Pat, let us get up and go home.

PAT. You're at home now.

MARIE. I'm not at home.

Pause.

MARIE. And it's true what they say.

PAT. What's that?

MARIE. Milk's twice as thick over there son, twice as thick. Have yi been over?

PAT. No.

MARIE. Yiv no been over.

PAT. No.

MARIE. Och, that's a shame. Yi should go.

PAT. What about you?

MARIE. Me?

PAT. What about you? Have you been over?

MARIE. I wasn't down the stairs twice in three years, but to the hospital, never mind to Ireland.

PAT. You should go back.

MARIE. Aye.

PAT. It's nice there.

MARIE. Aye.

PAT. Fine.

MARIE. Aye.

PAT. Not like Glasgow.

MARIE. No, not like Glasgow.

PAT. No.

MARIE. If you like it so well why don't you go over for a holiday.

PAT. Aye, a holiday would be a fine thing.

Silence.

MARIE. You should be ashamed of yersel. Where've you been? Leaving me lying here like an old dog, that lump doesn't do anything. The worry yiv caused me. Not

knowing if you were murdered or mamed or in an accident.
You an yer wife an boys. Not a word. I haven't been able t'
move I've been so sick wi worry, I've worried me eyes
away an ma insides, then comin back out o' the blue as if it
were only yesterday you went outside t' get a pint o' milk.

Silence. The mother then puts on the radio.

A wee frame is what yi bring back.

Not even a photograph.

Silence. She puts the radio off.

Sit here so's I can see yi.

She handles his face and then slaps him weakly.

Yiv no changed a bit. Still as handsome. After yer mother.
How's me hair?

PAT. It's nice.

MARIE. It's no a mess.

PAT. No.

MARIE. Pass me that mirror there. If I'd known yi were
comin' I would've had it done.

PAT. No, it's fine.

MARIE. Look at me now.

PAT. It suits you.

MARIE. There's a wee girl that comes round an' does it for
me, washes it, burns ma scalp, an then gives it a wee cut an
blow dry. She's not a looker.

PAT. Isn't she?

MARIE. No, you would a thought that in that business yi
would have to be a looker. Not pretty at all. Not pretty
enough for the boys around here. Not pretty enough for you.

PAT. No?

MARIE. No. Not pretty enough for a handsome man like you.
Getting something she's not good enough for.

PAT *gets up.*

MARIE. Where are yi going?

PAT *pauses.*

PAT. To the toilet.

MARIE. Oh, the toilet. Mind the seat.

PAT *leaves.* PAT *returns.*

MARIE. Aye, aye, aye.

PAT. You've got some damp in the toilet.

MARIE. Damp.

PAT. Aye. Around the window.

MARIE. Oh well.

PAT. Shall I phone the council? I could do it now.

MARIE. You'd have more luck phoning St Peter.

PAT. You need to get it seen to.

MARIE. Don't bother yer head.

Silence.

MARIE. Aye, maybe yi could gie them a wee ring, yi were always good wi words, weren't yi.

PAT. I was okay.

MARIE. You were more than okay.

PAT. I was better at other things.

MARIE. Always good wi words. I remember a wee card yi wrote t' me when yi were a wee boy an' what a poem yi wrote in it.

PAT. Did I?

MARIE. Aye, yi did. Do yi no remember?

PAT. No.

MARIE. Yi must be as old as me forgetting things. A Valentine's card it was.

PAT. St Valentine's.

MARIE. Yi always used t' send me a St Valentine's, every fourteenth of February.

PAT. I remember now.

MARIE. I wish I'd known that, I thought he was out with the old drink.

PAT. I made them for you.

MARIE. Aye, yi did.

PAT. Drew little pictures.

MARIE. Oh, aye, yi were good wi words.

PAT. Pictures of hearts.

MARIE. That schooling. Talented. That's what I told everyone. Talented. When I went round t' the priests or the teachers they all said the same thing. Talented boy.

PAT. Did they?

MARIE. Oh yes, so warm with praise they were. They said that boy could be a doctor. Those lovely poems.

PAT. The poems weren't very good.

MARIE. What a thing t' say.

PAT. Have you still got them?

MARIE. Oh aye, I'm sure they're around somewhere, packed up under the bed or in the spare room. It's a shame yi wasted what gifts God gave yi.

PAT. I haven't.

MARIE. Wasted a gift for words.

PAT. No.

MARIE. No? Even the priest said so. A doctor. I was dying.

Pause.

The fall I took there, I thought I'd never open an eye again. Half dead. You won't die he said. I'd say to him, what d'yi keep me alive for?

Silence. JACK *returns.*

MARIE. Where've yi been?

JACK. You know fine well where I've been.

MARIE. Where?

JACK. Out.

MARIE. Out?

JACK. Aye, out is what I said.

PAT. Is it cold out?

JACK. It's cold enough anyhow.

PAT. Is the wind still up?

JACK. Aye. It blows right through.

MARIE. What are yi sitting down for?

JACK. What sort o' question's that.

MARIE. The boy hasn't had a cup of tea or anything yet.

PAT. I'm okay.

MARIE. You were just saying how's you were wanting a cup of tea with some milk. Did yi get the milk?

JACK. No.

MARIE. No?

JACK. Aye. No. I forgot.

MARIE. Forgot.

JACK. Aye.

MARIE. Yi were only gone half an hour.

JACK. I forgot.

MARIE. I bet yi didn't forget t' go to the pub for a drink. No, of course yi didn't forget that. But yer quick enough t' forget t' buy some milk for yer son t' have a cup o' tea.

JACK. Och, weesht will yi.

MARIE. Away wi any other woman when yi should be at work. Taking her drink. Imagine someone else being in bed wi him. He's got some cheek on him.

PAT. It's okay.

MARIE. Aye, you tell him it's okay. Make him feel better.

JACK *gets up.*

MARIE. An' where are yi going now?

PAT. Sit down Dad.

JACK. T' get yer milk.

MARIE. Och, there's no point gettin' it now.

Pause.

MARIE. Did yi see anyone?

JACK. Who would I see?

MARIE. On the street.

JACK. No.

MARIE. Did yi see anyone when yi were out walking?

JACK. Aye.

MARIE. Who?

JACK. That young boy from downstairs.

MARIE. Which one?

JACK. The young one with the baby. You don't know him.

MARIE. I do.

JACK. When 'ave yi seen him?

MARIE. I see him from the window.

JACK. Aye.

MARIE. A lovely lad he is. You should have a talk with him. He's a father. He's daft for it. All he wants to do is nurse the baby.

Silence.

PAT. Do you not wear a hat when you go out?

JACK. What d' I need a hat fir.

PAT. To keep yer head warm.

JACK. Ma head's warm enough.

PAT. Aye. Did you put a bet on?

JACK. Aye.

PAT. Did yi win?

JACK. Did I win? No, I didn't win at all.

PAT. O well.

JACK. Passes the time anyway.

PAT. Aye.

MARIE. What time is it now Jack?

JACK. Twelve o'clock.

MARIE. Twelve o'clock is it.

JACK. Aye.

MARIE. What's it like having a sister Pat?

JACK. He doesn't have a sister.

MARIE. He does. A grand big sister. I watch them from the window walking together an' holding their wee hands in a knot.

JACK. Ti heng wi yi, a sister.

MARIE. Walking with her next t'a pram and that wee baby in all.

PAT. I don't have a sister.

MARIE. Aye, yi do.

PAT. That would mean you had a daughter.

MARIE. A daughter?

PAT. Aye.

Silence.

PAT. Is she alright?

JACK. Aye. Leave her be.

PAT. Mum.

JACK. Leave her be.

He looks at the paper.

PAT. What's in the paper?

JACK. News.

PAT. Anything interesting?

JACK. No. There's been a murder.

PAT. A murder.

JACK. Aye. A murder's what I said.

PAT. Where?

JACK. Out in Kilmarnock.

PAT. Kilmarnock.

JACK. Back in the war and before the war people didn't just stab each other, people had some work, not everyone, and even though there wasn't much choice you knew what t' expect and you knew a good day when yi had one and a good night's sleep too.

Pause.

PAT. D' yi watch the football?

JACK. What would I want t' watch the football for?

PAT. Well. Is there anything I can do?

JACK. Sit where yi are.

PAT. Nothing needing done around the house.

MARIE. Pat said he was going t' phone the council.

PAT. Yes, I did.

JACK. What the heng does he need t' phone the council for.

PAT. I noticed some damp in the bathroom.

JACK. It's no doing any harm.

PAT. I could phone the council an' get them round.

JACK. Some price they charge for that.

PAT. They don't charge anything.

JACK. I can't pay for that.

PAT. They shouldn't charge.

MARIE. Jack, listen t' him.

JACK. I'll phone them masel.

MARIE. Yi never will.

PAT. I'll phone.

JACK. Will yi sit where yi are.

MARIE. Jack.

PAT. Is the number in the book?

JACK. Aye.

PAT *leaves.*

MARIE. Shoutin' at that boy like that. Is it any wonder we never see him. Sittin' there smellin' o' whiskey. The state o yi. The sight of yi. No afford it. Aye, is it no wonder.

Pause. JACK *looks at his watch. He gets up and gives* MARIE *her pills, she drinks them down with water.*

Act Three

As before.

PAT. That's sorted then, they said they'd be round a week Monday.

MARIE. What about that then.

JACK. Aye.

MARIE. You always did get things done straight away. Not like him.

PAT. It's nothing, just a call.

MARIE. Aye, just a call. Who was it you spoke to?

PAT. A woman.

MARIE. Young?

PAT. I don't know.

MARIE. Was she nice sounding?

PAT. Well . . .

MARIE. They should always have someone nice sounding answering the phone.

JACK. What the heng difference does it make what they sound like.

MARIE. What would you know.

JACK. I know that it makes no difference.

MARIE. A nice sounding woman on the end of the phone.

JACK. Och . . .

MARIE. That Shona Docherty had a lovely sounding voice. Do you remember her Jack?

JACK. What the heng would I remember her for.

MARIE. Lovely dark hair she had and green eyes.

JACK. Aye, I remember her.

MARIE. A lovely girl, you remember her Pat?

PAT. Aye, I do.

MARIE. What a crush she had on you.

PAT. Yes. I remember well.

MARIE. She's got herself a husband now and children, would you believe.

PAT. Has she?

MARIE. Oh yes, a husband, a grand man. Been so short. A nice wife she woulda made.

Pause.

What does he do Jack? Shona's fella?

JACK. He's a builder.

MARIE. A builder.

JACK. Aye.

PAT. That's good. Are they happy?

MARIE. Happy. Aye. You missed a good one there. You should a' sent her a Valentine's card, not yer old Mum.

PAT. She wasn't ma type.

MARIE. Got three lovely wee girls.

JACK. Wee girls.

MARIE. The way she loved you.

JACK. They'd be women now.

MARIE. You don't find that very often.

JACK. Wi their own children.

MARIE. Aye, getting Valentines o' their own. Jack?

JACK. Aye.

MARIE. How long is it now to Valentine's?

JACK. Och, five months.

MARIE. Five months, when will that be then?

JACK. February.

MARIE. February. February what?

JACK. February fourteenth.

MARIE. Aye. I remember that day well enough. Children of her own. Grandchildren even.

Silence. MARIE starts to get up, she rises very slowly and supports herself on the surrounding surfaces and drags herself slowly out of the room.

PAT. What are you doing now?

JACK. What am I doing now, I'm sitting here holding a stick.

Pause.

All ma pals are dead. What am I going to do? Look into the fire. Not able to run about the same as I used to. When I got here I could jump over this house. Now I'm not able to walk.

Pause.

Aye, the old legs is away.

PAT. Has Mum been keeping well?

JACK. She's well enough. Here.

PAT. What?

JACK. Here.

JACK puts some money in PAT's hand.

PAT. What's that?

JACK. Take it.

PAT. I don't need it.

JACK. Take it.

PAT. Thanks.

PAT *gets up and looks out the window.*

PAT. Do you have a sleep in the afternoon?

JACK. Who, me?

PAT. Aye.

JACK. No, not at all.

PAT. She sleeps a lot.

JACK. She was sleeping before you got here.

Pause.

Good gracious I'm not tired. I can go out anytime.

Pause.

PAT. The garden looks nice.

JACK. Aye.

PAT. Do you do it?

JACK. What would I be doing gardening?

PAT. You used to like it.

JACK. The man down stairs does it.

PAT. He does a good job. Could you not help him?

JACK. Ach.

PAT. Do you remember the two window boxes we used to have on the veranda?

JACK. Aye.

PAT. Two little gardens.

JACK. Aye.

PAT. You used to enjoy planting things in them. It's a shame they couldn't have given you an allotment.

JACK. Aye, I tell yi, I wouldn't want t' be out digging in the evening after spending all ma days digging.

PAT. No, I don't suppose you would.

JACK. No. I wouldn't.

PAT. But it would be a different sort of digging.

JACK. Aye.

PAT. For yersel.

JACK. Aye. Maybe.

PAT. I see you've got some pills as well.

JACK. Aye.

PAT. What are these for?

JACK. Sleeping.

PAT. Do you not sleep?

JACK. What would make me tired, I'm sitting in the house all day. You need work to be tired.

PAT. You should go out for a longer walk.

JACK. Och, t' heng wi that.

PAT. Was that your stick by the door?

JACK. Aye.

PAT. How long have you had that?

JACK. Six years.

Silence.

PAT. She's a long time in there.

JACK. Aye.

PAT. Should yi no check she's alright.

JACK. T'heng I will, I'm fed up seein'.

Pause.

PAT. Does Mum sleep?

JACK. I don't know what she does. She was sleepin' some o' the time.

Silence.

Aye well, and how are things with you?

The voice of MARIE *shouting 'Jack' is heard.* JACK *gets up and leaves the room.* PAT *looks around the kitchen.* MARIE *comes back into the room.*

MARIE. Here.

PAT. What.

MARIE. Here.

PAT. Mum.

MARIE. Take it.

PAT. I don't need it.

MARIE. Take the money. He'll only spend it on drink. Take it before yer father comes back.

PAT. Thanks.

MARIE. And look after yersel now, take good food, don't run yersel down and fall into something.

JACK *comes back in.*

MARIE. There. Are yi not going t' make the lad a cup of tea?

JACK. He doesn't want any tea.

MARIE. Give him some of what you've been havin'. Aye. Don't think I don't know. Above the boiler he keeps a wee bottle. He doesn't think I know about it. I know. I got the priest t' have a look on one of his visits and he told me what I already knew. An then the priest coming round and the cleaner and do you not think they don't smell it on yi. What d' yi think they think of me. Does that not enter yer head? And him used t' be so hard working as well. I hope you keep away from it, look after yersel, take good food . . .

PAT. Yes.

MARIE. Aye, that's my boy. Do I have t' get up and make it masel?

JACK. Stay where yi are.

PAT. Dad, it's okay.

JACK. Never mind.

He puts the kettle on.

MARIE. You're not going to use those mugs.

JACK. No.

MARIE. Aye. Good. And how's that wife of yours now?

PAT. I don't know.

MARIE. No? Well. An' them wee boys?

Pause.

What d' yi expect. An' look at yi now.

Pause.

PAT. I'm nearly as old as you.

MARIE. Aye, yer not far off. Old enough t' be a grandfather.

PAT. Aye, I am.

MARIE. Running off wi that.

Silence.

What weather are yi havin' where yi are?

PAT. The same as here.

MARIE. Always when yi go travellin' put somethin' extra on yi. Always have a cup o' tea when yi can. Jack. Is that tea ready?

JACK. We've no milk.

MARIE. Did yi no get the milk?

JACK. You know fine well I didn't.

MARIE. Did yi no.

JACK. No.

MARIE. What about the lad's tea? Go out an get some milk Jack.

PAT. Sit down Dad. I'll get some.

JACK. You'll no do anything.

MARIE. Let him get the milk if he wants some in his tea.

PAT *gets up, he puts on his jacket and leaves.* MARIE *and* JACK *sit there.*

MARIE. There's that wee lad wi his sister.

JACK. Aye.

MARIE. He'll need to put more on than that, look at him with his hair wet. Have you not put on the dinner Jack?

JACK. It's too early for dinner.

MARIE. Oh, is it now.

JACK. Aye.

Silence.

MARIE. Is it not night yet?

JACK. No, it's no night.

MARIE. I thought it would be night by now.

JACK. Well, it's not.

MARIE. Sure it's not night, I can still see the tree.

Silence.

MARIE. The sun's starting to shine now.

JACK. It was out earlier.

MARIE. Aye, but it went away. Aye, there, the sun's shining now.

Silence.

MARIE. Did yi see anyone else when yi were out?

JACK. Who would I see?

MARIE. Aye, who would you see.

Silence.

Fade to black.

ONE GOOD BEATING

Linda McLean

For my father, Hugh McLean, 1933–1998

Characters

ROBERT, *father*

ELAINE, *daughter*

STEPHEN, *son*

ELAINE *and* STEPHEN *are standing outside the coal shed.*
The coal shed is sideways on with the front door facing the left.
The wall facing us is cut away so we can see into it. Inside the
shed sits ROBERT, *their father, listening to them.*

ELAINE (*whispering*). I want to hit him.

STEPHEN. Me too.

ELAINE. No. Really. I want to hit him. Hard.

STEPHEN. What? You mean . . . go in there . . . and give him
    one.

ELAINE. More than one.

STEPHEN. How many?

ELAINE. I don't know.

STEPHEN. Three? Five.

ELAINE. I don't know. Till it's over. Till I'm done. Can I?

STEPHEN. It's not for me to say.

ELAINE. You would have to hold him. I couldn't do it myself.

STEPHEN. It's a bit . . .

ELAINE. What?

STEPHEN. A bit . . . sick. Elaine.

ELAINE. I feel sick. Don't you? Didn't today make you feel
    sick?

STEPHEN. Not sick exactly.

ELAINE. What then?

STEPHEN. Sad, I suppose.

ELAINE. Well I'll hold him while you cry if you hold him while I give him a good thumping.

STEPHEN. But he never hit you.

ELAINE. Don't do that.

STEPHEN. What?

ELAINE. The past is the past. Refuse to discuss it.

STEPHEN. I don't understand. I thought the past was why we put him in there.

ELAINE. No.

STEPHEN. It's why I put him in there. See how he likes it.

ELAINE. Well you'd better bugger off then. You'll be useless.

STEPHEN. I'm a lot stronger than you.

ELAINE. If he thinks for a minute that you're stuck in the past he'll beat you. He'll talk rings round you. Explanations. Justifications. No. Ignore any remarks about the past.

STEPHEN. Why did you do it then?

ELAINE. We did it.

STEPHEN. Yes, but . . . I told you. I thought it was for/

ELAINE. /I'm angry. That's why I wanted him in there. Because I'm angry. Today. Now. This minute. Not then. Not way back then. Now. I'm bloody raging at him. I want to hit him. Hard.

STEPHEN. Yes.

ELAINE. When I just think of his face I want to smash it.

STEPHEN. Yes.

ELAINE. When I think of that . . . that . . . bloody box.

STEPHEN. Bloody awful box.

ELAINE. Yes. So. Can I?

STEPHEN. . . . Yes.

ELAINE. You'll hold him?

STEPHEN. I want to hit him too.

ELAINE. O.K. but me first.

STEPHEN. He's a . . .

ELAINE. He's a bastard.

STEPHEN. A bad tempered old bastard.

ELAINE. He deserves a good kicking.

STEPHEN. A bloody nose.

ELAINE. She was too good for him.

STEPHEN. Far too good. Bloody bastard.

ELAINE. Bloody nose.

STEPHEN. Good bloody kicking.

ELAINE. Get him then.

STEPHEN. Aye. Get him.

ELAINE. Come on then.

STEPHEN. Come on.

They run at the coal shed and pull back the bolts to open the door.

ROBERT is sitting on the ground huddled in a ball with his hands wrapped over his head.

ROBERT. Don't hit me. Please don't hit me.

STEPHEN. Shit.

ELAINE. Come on then.

STEPHEN. Shit.

ROBERT. I beg you. Please. Don't hurt me.

ELAINE. Hold him.

STEPHEN. Fuck.

ELAINE grabs hold of him and shakes him.

ELAINE. Come on. Pull yourself together.

STEPHEN. Look at him.

ELAINE. It's an act.

STEPHEN. He's pathetic.

ELAINE. It's an act.

STEPHEN. I can't.

ELAINE. Bugger off then.

She pushes him out of the shed. ROBERT *unfolds his arms and looks up at her. He winks.*

ELAINE. You old bastard.

She kicks him and leaves. STEPHEN *is sitting outside, head in hands. She slaps him.*

STEPHEN. Hey.

ELAINE. You bastard.

STEPHEN. I couldn't.

ELAINE. You know what he did? Soon as you were out of there? He winked at me. Bloody well winked at me. That was you. You let him do that to me. You bastard.

STEPHEN. He was crying.

ELAINE. Crying my arse. He's laughing at you. Go on. Take a look. Laughing.

She shoves him.

ELAINE. Go on.

STEPHEN *pulls open the door to the coal bunker and* ROBERT *is smiling at him.*

STEPHEN. I'll hit him now. Come on.

ELAINE. Aw shut the door. Before the smell gets to me. Have you shit yourself, father?

STEPHEN. I can. I can hit him now.

ELAINE *shuts the door and bolts it.*

ELAINE. All you had to do was hold him. Hold him till I hit him. It was that simple. And quick. I would've hit him. Then you would've hit him. And that would've been it. One good beating and we would've been finished.

STEPHEN. I can do it now.

ELAINE. Do you know what you've done?

STEPHEN. We can still do it.

ELAINE. No we can't. The moment's gone. The moment when we could have beaten him. A good beating. Is gone.

STEPHEN. We can still beat him.

ELAINE. He beat us.

STEPHEN. But . . . you kicked him. You've done your bit.

ELAINE. That was different. I kicked him because he beat me. And I'm a bad loser.

STEPHEN. He winked?

ELAINE. Yes.

STEPHEN. Bastard.

ELAINE. Yes.

STEPHEN. I should never have fallen for all that begging and crying.

ELAINE. No.

STEPHEN. So what do we do now?

ELAINE. Exactly.

STEPHEN. I'm going to phone Holly.

ELAINE. No.

STEPHEN. Why not? I need to tell her. She doesn't even know.

ELAINE. Don't phone her yet. Till we know. What we're going to do.

STEPHEN. Well I'll need to phone her sometime.

ELAINE. We'll all need to phone some time. But not now. Not yet.

STEPHEN. What are you going to do?

ELAINE. We.

STEPHEN. Yeah yeah. We.

ELAINE. I don't know. I don't suppose you can make tea?

STEPHEN. Of course I can make tea. What kind of remark is that?

ELAINE. Well I don't know whether you make tea or not. Maybe somebody else in your house makes the tea. Maybe what you make is piss water.

STEPHEN. Just because I couldn't hit him doesn't mean I can't make tea.

ELAINE. Good.

STEPHEN. Right. I make good tea.

ELAINE. Well make it then.

STEPHEN. Don't.

ELAINE. What?

STEPHEN. Don't do that.

ELAINE. Do what?

STEPHEN. Order me about. I'm in this too, you know. It's not just you. She was my mother as well.

ELAINE. I'm pleased to hear it.

STEPHEN. I loved her too.

ELAINE. Don't get upset. Not yet. Look, I'm sorry. I was just . . . I'm a bit . . . thrown.

STEPHEN. O.K. Well. Do you want tea?

ELAINE. Yes. Please.

STEPHEN. Right. I'll get it then.

STEPHEN *leaves.*

ROBERT. 'Lainey. 'Lainey. What are you doing hen? What are you thinking? Hey. You used to be ma wee girl. Remember, 'Lainey.

Lay Lainey
Ower the glen
Daddy's pet
An Mammy's hen.

Remember 'Lainey? On the swing? Come on. You remember.

ELAINE. I don't remember anything.

ROBERT. Of course you do. Up the Cathkin Braes on a Sunday. 'Swing high, Daddy. Higher.' And up we went. Just you and me.

ELAINE. I don't remember.

ROBERT. Let me out, Elaine.

ELAINE. No.

ROBERT. There's a terrible smell in here.

ELAINE. Good.

ROBERT. Rot. Some kind of rot. Like . . . dead mouse.

ELAINE. Maybe there is a dead mouse. Place has never been cleaned.

ROBERT. And you're a clean girl aren't you? You like things clean.

ELAINE. Yes I do.

ROBERT. My nice clean girl. Honest and straight, that's my girl. No sides. No behind the back dirty dealing. Eh, Elaine?

ELAINE. So?

ROBERT. So. How you going to square this one up? Eh? I'd like to hear that? Locked your Da in the coal shed. The stinking coal shed. For why? For a joke? Ha ha. Kicked him an all? Not so funny joke. You know how it'll look, don't you?

ELAINE. I don't care.

ROBERT. It'll look like revenge.

ELAINE. It's not revenge.

ROBERT. Revenge for the times YOU sat here.

ELAINE. It's not revenge.

ROBERT. In the dark. And you were afraid of the dark, weren't you, 'Lainey?

ELAINE. I'm not afraid of the dark.

ROBERT. No? You were.

ELAINE. I like the dark.

ROBERT. First thing you did when you got out was jump straight into a bath. Scrub yourself clean.

ELAINE. There's comfort in the dark.

ROBERT. Comfort in it? You might be right.

ELAINE. And I like the smell of coal.

ROBERT. There's none of that here. No honest black coal. Dead something. That's what there is now. Dead something. Puppy maybe.

ELAINE *thumps the door of the coal shed.*

ROBERT. Maybe not. Maybe it's mouse.

ELAINE. You didn't even give her a proper funeral.

ROBERT. The puppy?

ELAINE. Don't act smart. My mother. I'm talking about my mother.

ROBERT. She was my wife.

ELAINE. A rotten cardboard box.

ROBERT. She was a rotten wife.

ELAINE. You're a mean old bastard.

ROBERT. Not at all.

ELAINE. You are so.

ROBERT. Your mother was an environmentalist, Elaine. Never out of bloody bottle banks and recycling dumps. She would've been happy with the cardboard box.

ELAINE. You never even told anybody she was dead.

ROBERT. I told you.

ELAINE. This morning. When I got here.

ROBERT. I told Stephen.

ELAINE. Was it the money? Were you scared people would be looking for a meal. Or a drink.

ROBERT. Tut tut. Now now. They don't cost nothing these cardboard coffins, you know.

ELAINE. Bloody cheapest thing you could get.

ROBERT. Not by a long chalk. There were at least two cheaper – not to mention the recyclable bag.

ELAINE. Even you wouldn't have buried her in a bin bag.

ROBERT. It's not a bin bag. It's a highly sophisticated piece of modern technology. Biodegrades in rhythm with Mother Nature. And I would've but they were out of stock. They're very popular you know. All the rage. But it was going to take two weeks to order another one. Couldn't have her hanging about the place for two weeks.

ELAINE. You're disgusting.

ROBERT. Not that you'd have noticed any difference. Your mother has been silent for so long now that sometimes I forgot she was there. But two weeks. She would've went off. And you know me, Elaine, I canny abide bad meat.

ELAINE. You'd think. This once. You might have not let her down.

ROBERT. Aye.

ELAINE. You might have done this one thing properly.

ROBERT. She did like things done properly. Didn't she?

ELAINE. What's wrong with that?

ROBERT. So do it then.

ELAINE. What?

ROBERT. Whatever you're going to do. Do it properly and get it by.

ELAINE. Aye you'd like that, wouldn't you? Short sharp shock. Well, I don't think I will. I've no made up my mind, mark you, but I think I'll let you sweat it out a bit.

ROBERT. Smacks of petty revenge. I always thought you were capable of greater things. I hate to see you petty. Your mother was petty.

ELAINE. She was not.

ROBERT. Oh Christ, Elaine. She counted the bloody toast. There I'd be. Dipping my toast in my egg. And I'd reach for another bit. Just to mop it up. 'Two,' she'd say. 'That's your second slice.' And even when I told her to belt up she'd still mouth it. Couldny even get peace to eat my breakfast.

ELAINE. Your fault. Your fault. You always took more than your fair share. We'd have had nothing if she hadn't counted it.

ROBERT. So you remember something then?

ELAINE. . . . .

ROBERT. She wouldn't have been happy about this.

ELAINE. Happy? She's delirious. Can you not hear her?

STEPHEN *comes back with tea.*

ELAINE (*loud*). Oh a cup of tea. Lovely.

STEPHEN. What?

She nudges him.

ELAINE. And toasted cheese and tomato.

There's no toast.

I bet he'd like some.

STEPHEN. D'you think so?

ELAINE. Would you like some toasted cheese Father?

ROBERT. Piss off.

ELAINE. He doesn't want any.

ROBERT. You haven't got any.

ELAINE. 'Course we have and we're going to eat it while you sit in there and think about your actions.

ROBERT. Liar.

ELAINE. And then, when you're ready, you can come in and apologise and we'll say no more about it. Are you ready to apologise?

ROBERT. . . .

ELAINE. I don't hear you.

ROBERT. I AM sorry.

ELAINE *and* STEPHEN *don't expect this.* STEPHEN *makes a move towards the shed.* ELAINE *holds him back.*

ELAINE. Say that again.

ROBERT. I never made you say it twice.

ELAINE. But you made me explain what . . . For what?

ROBERT. What?

ELAINE. What are you sorry for?

ROBERT. That all my efforts to turn you two into decent human beings were obviously wasted. You're useless. And I had such hopes. Especially you, Elaine.

ELAINE. You're sick.

ROBERT. I'm telling you. There is nothing more disappointing in this life than watching your children fail. Naw. That's no quite true. Sex with your mother. Now there was/

STEPHEN. Shutup.

He bangs on the shed.

STEPHEN. You better shutup. How come, even when he's in there. Even when he's . . . how can we shut his mouth? I want to shut him up.

ELAINE. Shut him up then.

STEPHEN. Shut his mouth.

ELAINE. Stick it shut.

STEPHEN. Well and truly.

ELAINE. Shut.

STEPHEN. For good.

ELAINE. Stuck.

STEPHEN. Shut.

ELAINE. Right.

STEPHEN. Right.

She goes out.

ROBERT. This was her idea, wasn't it, son?

STEPHEN. . . .

ROBERT. You would never have done this yourself.

STEPHEN. . . .

ROBERT. She talked you into it, didn't she?

STEPHEN. . . .

ROBERT. She can be very persuasive.

STEPHEN. . . .

ROBERT. But she'll leave you to carry the can. Always did.

STEPHEN. How come you never saw that before? How come I was always the one that got belted while she got a hug?

ROBERT. She had me twisted round her wee finger. You saw that. Besides. I don't hold wi hitting women.

STEPHEN. . . .

ROBERT. If you open the door I won't do anything.

STEPHEN. No.

ROBERT. I'll just slip off.

STEPHEN. No.

ROBERT. You can tell her I overpowered you.

STEPHEN. No.

ROBERT. Whatever you like. Make something up.

STEPHEN. I can't.

ROBERT. Naw. Right enough. You never had an original idea in that thick skull of yours. Did you son?

STEPHEN. So you say.

ROBERT. Take after your mother. Always have. Weak genes.

STEPHEN. Shut it.

ROBERT. Do you not want to talk about your mother?

STEPHEN. I mean it.

ROBERT. She was a beautiful woman. Was she not?

STEPHEN. . . .

ROBERT. Ah. How would you know? You never saw the best of her. When I first met her she was . . . a wee cracker. God she was brilliant. Her eyes shone and her cheeks glowed. She was perfect to hold. Soft and round in all the right places.

STEPHEN. . . .

ROBERT. Not like women these days. Aw thin and pointy. Melt right into her, you could.

STEPHEN. . . .

ROBERT. You loved it, when you were a wean. Couldny get you off her. Suck her to death, you would've.

STEPHEN. . . .

ROBERT. Even after the milk dried up.

STEPHEN. . . .

ROBERT. Are the tears tripping you yet?

STEPHEN. You're a bastard.

ROBERT. So your sister tells me.

STEPHEN. She's grieving.

ROBERT. We're all grieving, son.

STEPHEN. We've just lost our mother.

ROBERT. And I've just lost my new found freedom. I had plans you know.

STEPHEN. I'm sure you did.

ROBERT. How long are you going to keep me in here?

STEPHEN. Till you rot.

ROBERT. Elaine'll never go through with it.

STEPHEN. Elaine hates you.

ROBERT. Nah. She's just annoyed. She'll come round.

STEPHEN. Even more than I hate you.

ROBERT. It's temporary. Elaine knows I loved her.

STEPHEN. There was nothing to love.

ROBERT. That's why she's stronger than you.

STEPHEN. Nothing.

ROBERT. And weaker. In my hands.

STEPHEN. Don't be so sure. She'll never forgive you for today.

ROBERT. There have been worse days.

STEPHEN. We're finished with you. Both of us.

ROBERT. Liar. If you were finished with me you wouldn't have shut me up in here. But here I am. If you were finished with me you would be gone. But here you are. You are stuck.

STEPHEN. We can go any time.

ROBERT. I can go at any time.

STEPHEN. No. You are stuck.

ROBERT. I can get out of here any time I like. The game is no when. The game is how.

ELAINE *comes back with a roll of tape.* ROBERT *hears her.*

ROBERT. And don't let Elaine find you weeping. She canny abide it either. Tears. Sentimentality.

ELAINE *signals shh.*

ROBERT. She's never shown me one moment of sympathy. Ma whole life. She's hard.

STEPHEN. She's not hard. She's hurt.

ROBERT. Is that what she says? Hurt? Naw. Naw. I was in the army son. I met a lot of hurt men. Met a lot of hard men. None of them as hard as her.

STEPHEN. If you hurt people often enough they toughen up.

ROBERT. What happened to you then? How is it you're still soft?

STEPHEN. I'm not soft.

ROBERT. You must be joking. You're plasticine, son. Not like my girl. She takes after me. She even looks like me, do you not think?

ELAINE *shakes her head but* STEPHEN *looks more closely.*

ROBERT. Aye. Everybody thought she looked like her mother
but she doesn't. That sneer she's got. That's mine. That look
in her eyes when she decides to rip your heart out. Mine an
all. You, Stephen. You look like your mother.

ELAINE. Don't start that.

STEPHEN. Start what?

ELAINE. Leave him alone.

STEPHEN. No. Start what? What are you talking about? I don't
need you to fight my battles. In case you never noticed
I grew up.

ROBERT. You see, hen. You see what happens when you try to
help. The weak are always like that. Waiting for an opportunity to snap at your ankles.

His mother was the same.

ELAINE. My mother was not . . . (*weak*).

My mother was . . . (*weak*).

ROBERT. Weak weak weak.

I never could see myself in you, son. Not a hair. Not a
thought. Not even in the gaps between your thoughts. I swear
to God you're somebody else's.

STEPHEN. You bad bastard.

ROBERT. You have to admit, there's no similarity. And a man
starts to think. You know?

Here's me. I'm a powerful man. I could expect to pass that
on. Eh? And there's you. Nothing but a big sooky wean.
A big sooky wean that loved his mammy. Had to be
dragged to school every day. Waa waaa. Eh son? Eh? You
start every day. Waa waaa. Eh son? Eh? You start to think.

STEPHEN. That's it. That's enough.

ROBERT. How come you've no weans, Stephen? You and that
Holly? Yous are getting on a bit. Leaving it late. Bit thin
and pointy for ma taste, that Holly. Bet she's the boss, eh?

If she wanted weans you'd have them. Am I right? Maybe
no. Ho. Stephen. Trouble in the willy department? Is that it?
No hard enough? Plasticine willy an all?

STEPHEN *strides to the shed and pulls open the door.*
ROBERT *is standing right there, looking at him.*

ROBERT. Please don't hurt me. I beg you.

STEPHEN. Shutup.

ROBERT. Make me. Make me.

STEPHEN. I'm your son.

ROBERT. I know. (*To* ELAINE.) He's waiting here for the
chance to forgive me. Did you know that? If I put my arms
around him and tell him I'm sorry, truly sorry, he'll forgive
me. After aw the beatings and bad mouthing, aw the nights
he spent in this crap hole of a shed. He's prepared to forgive
me. He might even forget. Can you believe that? Five
minutes from now he could be saying 'My father belted me
but it never did me any harm.' Don't you find that amazing?
Bloody amazing. Would you forgive me Elaine?

ELAINE. Fuck off.

ROBERT. See. Do you see that son? And do you know what?
It's her forgiveness I want. I don't give a toss about yours.
I'm sorry. But I don't. I couldn't give a tuppenny damn
whether you forgave me or not. In fact, I'd rather you didny.

STEPHEN *punches him in the stomach. Not that hard. And
shuts the door. He's shaking.*

STEPHEN. What? What are you looking at me like that for?

ELAINE. I don't understand why you care.

STEPHEN. I can't help it.

ELAINE. But he treats you . . . worse than a dog.

STEPHEN. All I wanted from him . . . I wanted him to love
me. Why can he not love me? Am I not good enough?

ELAINE. It's just him. He's an animal. If he thinks you're
weak he has to prey on you. You can't be weak.

STEPHEN. But I'm not. Out there. I'm as tough as the rest of them. Really.

ELAINE. You were never tough, Stephen.

STEPHEN. I am.

ELAINE. You work in a library for Christsake.

STEPHEN. Oh what? That's not tough enough?

ELAINE. I didn't say that.

STEPHEN. You think because you work in a fancy office with consultants that you've cornered the market on toughness?

ELAINE. I run that office.

STEPHEN. You see. That matters to you. You run it. You're as bad as him sometimes.

ELAINE. Don't. This is what he wants. You and I to fight. Don't give it to him.

STEPHEN. I don't know what he wants. What do you want Dad? What do you really want?

ELAINE. Stephen, don't. Don't let him do this to you. Here. I'm going to tape his mouth. That'll shut him up. Give me a hand.

STEPHEN. Not before he tells me.

STEPHEN *opens the door of the shed once again.*

STEPHEN. What is it you want?

ROBERT. Shut the door.

STEPHEN. What is it you want from me?

ROBERT. Shut the fucking door.

STEPHEN. No. In fact. You can walk out it if you like.

ELAINE. Stephen.

ROBERT. Is that right Elaine. Can I go?

STEPHEN. I said you can go.

ROBERT. Elaine?

ELAINE. Answer him.

ROBERT. What?

ELAINE. Tell him what you want from him so he can stop turning himself inside out trying to be it.

ROBERT. It's pathetic.

ELAINE. Tell him.

STEPHEN. Tell me.

ROBERT. I canny.

STEPHEN. Tell me.

ROBERT. There's nothing to tell. I want nothing from you.

STEPHEN. That's a lie. Nothing I ever did was good enough. That's why you loved her.

ROBERT. Naw. Nothing you did was good enough because you were you. I don't like you.

STEPHEN. That's it?

ROBERT. I never did.

STEPHEN. You mean it didn't matter what I did?

ROBERT. Naw. I tried to tell you. But you kept coming back, like a wee puppy dug. It just annoyed me.

STEPHEN. But why d'you not like me?

ROBERT. Who knows?

STEPHEN. And I'm supposed to just live with that? Could you not try?

ROBERT. Elaine. For Jesus sake, this is pathetic, hen.

ELAINE. Let him finish.

ROBERT. He'll just get worse. I'll end up hurting him.

STEPHEN. Let me finish. What about Mum?

ROBERT. She loved you.

STEPHEN. No. I mean, did you love Mum?

ROBERT. I don't need to answer that, do I?

ELAINE. I think you should.

ROBERT. I don't know. I don't know what it means. I lived
wi her. I slept wi her. Wasny always brilliant but it was
enough. Did I love her? I don't know. She was a bit thick.
Like you, son.

STEPHEN. I'm not thick. I've got a brain.

ROBERT. Naw, naw. Thick - as in slow moving lava. Painful
to watch, sometimes. Predictable.

STEPHEN. And that's it? That's what I've got to take away
from here? That. And I can't change that.

ROBERT. Here's progress.

STEPHEN. Well, it's your loss.

ROBERT. I won't feel it.

STEPHEN w*alks away from the shed leaving the door
open.*

ROBERT. Shut the door.

ELAINE. Happy now? Is that what you wanted? You made
him say it, didn't you?

STEPHEN. Why don't YOU have any children, Elaine?

ELAINE. What?

STEPHEN. I know why I haven't got any. Because I'm too
scared. Too scared that I'll turn out like him. But why
haven't you?

ELAINE. I've no partner. You know that.

STEPHEN. You don't need one.

ELAINE. I have no lover.

STEPHEN. Why?

ELAINE. I don't know. Haven't found the right one I don't
suppose.

STEPHEN. Really?

ELAINE. Stephen? It's not my fault. It's him. Don't blame it on me.

STEPHEN. Doesn't it worry you that he does love you?

ELAINE. He doesn't love anybody except himself.

STEPHEN. I'm going home.

ELAINE. But we're not finished.

STEPHEN. I'm finished. Well and truly. I'm going home.

ELAINE. What about him?

STEPHEN. What about him?

ELAINE. We can't just leave him there.

STEPHEN. You do what you like. I'm off.

ELAINE. That's not fair. We put him in there together. We should see it through together.

STEPHEN. Didn't you hear him? There is no us. There is only you.

ELAINE. That's him. Not me.

STEPHEN. I can't do anything. You saw that. I have no power. You do what you have to.

ELAINE. Don't let him win now, Stephen. We've always seen it through because we were a team. Us against him. Don't let him win.

STEPHEN. You're kidding yourself on, Elaine.

ELAINE. I'm not.

STEPHEN. You fight him if you want. But understand that it's because you want to.

ELAINE. What do you mean?

STEPHEN. Has it ever occurred to you that maybe he's the only thing we've got in common? That if it wasn't for him there wouldn't be an us?

ELAINE. That's a lie. Come on. We have fun.

STEPHEN. When? What fun?

ELAINE. We have a laugh.

STEPHEN. WE don't have a laugh. You say very witty things about how stupid the man in the street is, how easy he is to con and I laugh because I'm glad it's not me you're talking about.

ELAINE. Stephen?

STEPHEN. You know what I think?

ELAINE. Those are funny stories. Everybody's got a funny story. You do it too.

STEPHEN. But you sound like him.

ELAINE. What?

STEPHEN. When you're telling your stories I see him – him belittling us – not you, never you – me and Mum. Making a fool of us.

ELAINE. They are just funny stories.

STEPHEN. It's what I see.

ELAINE. Why did you never tell me?

STEPHEN. I didn't know. It's only now I see you here. Still wanting to beat him. You can't walk away from it. Can you?

ELAINE. He deserves it.

STEPHEN. You enjoy it. Nobody else can beat you. Can they? You've tried and nobody comes up to quite his standard.

ELAINE. I have to beat him because he's wrong.

STEPHEN. Still?

ELAINE. If I don't fight him it means that what he did . . . to you . . . to Mum . . . it's all O.K. He can't get away with thinking it's O.K.

STEPHEN. It's over. He only does it for you now.

ELAINE. That's a lie. What about this morning? What about that? That was to get at you as well.

STEPHEN. I'm going home.

ELAINE. What does that mean, Stephen?

STEPHEN. It just means I'm going home.

ELAINE. For us? What does it mean for us?

   STEPHEN *walks away.*

ROBERT. Good riddance to bad rubbish.

ELAINE. Shutup. You miserable old pig.

ROBERT. So. What you gonny do now, 'Lainey?

ELAINE. I'm going home too.

ROBERT. But you're not finished.

ELAINE. I'm finished with you.

ROBERT. You have to let me out.

ELAINE. I don't need to let you out. The door's open.

ROBERT. I need your permission.

ELAINE. Piss off.

ROBERT. I'll stay here till you tell me.

ELAINE. You will not. You're too fond of your dinner.

ROBERT. I will. Your permission is the only thing I want.

ELAINE. I can't.

ROBERT. You can't just walk away from me.

ELAINE. Watch me.

   She walks.

ROBERT. You say you don't remember.

ELAINE. I don't.

ROBERT. But you will.

ELAINE. It's too depressing.

ROBERT. Not all of it.

She stops.

ELAINE. You killed my dog.

ROBERT. I hit her too hard. That was all.

She walks.

ROBERT. I love you Elaine.

ELAINE. Fuck off.

ROBERT. You loved me once.

ELAINE. I'm sorry for that.

ROBERT. You don't stop loving somebody.

She stops.

ELAINE. Yes you do.

ROBERT. Naw, hen. You just put it away somewhere till it's safe to bring it out and look at it.

She walks.

ROBERT. It's no for me. The permission. It's for you. It's a gift from me to you.

She stops.

ELAINE. Keep your gift. They always come with a price.

ROBERT. A free gift.

ELAINE. There's no such thing.

She walks.

ROBERT. Your mother then.

ELAINE. What about her?

ROBERT. You loved her. Right?

ELAINE. Of course.

ROBERT. Of course. Some day, when you're really grown up, you'll be able to take an honest look at her. Nobody's perfect.

She stops.

ELAINE. In comparison to you she was a bloody saint.

ROBERT. In comparison to me. But I know you. And come that day when you're pulling her apart and wondering why she didn't do more or how come she let this happen and that happen. That day. You'll start to think.

ELAINE. About what?

ROBERT. About who you are. Are you as good as her? As bad as me?

ELAINE. . . .

ROBERT. I just need your permission.

ELAINE *turns.*

ELAINE. I can't forgive you.

ROBERT. Who's asking?

ELAINE. And I don't want to see you.

ROBERT. Don't look then.

ELAINE. I mean . . . I'm not coming to visit. Don't come and visit me.

ROBERT. I don't go where I'm no wanted.

ELAINE. You're not wanted.

ROBERT. So.

ELAINE. What?

ROBERT. Can I come out?

ELAINE. . . .

ROBERT. Elaine.

ELAINE. Just . . .

ROBERT. Elai/

ELAINE. /Give me a minute. I need a minute.

ROBERT. . . .

ELAINE. Right.

ROBERT. Say the words.

ELAINE. . . .

ROBERT. Say it.

ELAINE. Come out then.

Black.

End.

THE VISITOR

Iain Crichton Smith

Characters

GEORGE

HELEN

HEINE

The Visitor

Night, GEORGE *is talking to a long mirror tilted slightly to make the scene look off-centre, a little odd.* HELEN *is sitting watching him.*

GEORGE. Rector, colleagues and indeed friends, I am standing here before you today because I have come to the end of a very long road. I might say weary road but I will not say it. In short, I have arrived at my retiral. Little did I think when I climbed that brae to the school forty years ago as a fresh faced young teacher that this day would ever come. Will that do dear, as a start?

HELEN. Yes, it will do well.

GEORGE. I know that Mr Harper had a few jokes in his speech but then I am not a natural jester.

HELEN. No, dear, you are not.

GEORGE. And after all it is a serious occasion. There are one or two things I would like to draw attention to.

HELEN. What are these, dear?

GEORGE. Well, I should like to see the return of gowns, for instance. I think they confer a dignity and . . .

A knock or ring at the door.

Who can that be at this time of night? Most odd.

HELEN. Indeed, dear.

GEORGE. Still, I shall have to answer it. Is the door locked, dear?

HELEN. Yes I am afraid it is.

GEORGE. Yes of course. It is eleven o'clock.

GEORGE goes to the door. After a while he comes in with a younger, energetic man, with a moustache.

HEINE. I am very sorry to intrude, sir, on you and your loyal wife, but I could not refrain from doing so when I read of your retiral in the local newspaper.

GEORGE. Why was that sir?

HEINE. Oh, I am sorry. Let me introduce myself. My name is Heine.

GEORGE. You are a German, sir?

HEINE. Not exactly so, Mr Burnett. Or rather that statement would have to be modified a little. It was in fact my landlady, Mrs Wilson, who pointed out the relevant paragraph in the newspaper under the heading FORTY YEARS YOUNG. She does not know you herself personally, sir, though she has seen you from a distance. But, to my tale. You see, sir, I was in your class and that little paragraph drew back a curtain for me, sir. You do not recognise me, sir? Madam? Of course, the ravages of time . . . but that often happens with me – I mean people not recognising me. You, madam, if I am not mistaken, taught Latin, amo amas amat, and you, sir – who does not know that? – taught English. I come to congratulate you, sir, on your retirement.

Ceremonies such as these
In spite of appearances may please.

GEORGE. I do not wish to be impolite, sir, but may I ask why you have come?

HEINE. To congratulate you, sir, to warmly congratulate you, sir, if one may be permitted a split infinitive. You see, I work in advertising, sir. An example of my rhymes would be:

Rover dog food is the best
For your dog if he is depressed.

It is of course not as good as Pope or indeed as my namesake, the great German poet, Heine, though of course he wrote in German.

HELEN *leans forward as if to speak but then, noticing a photograph,* HEINE *leaps up.*

HEINE. Will that be a photograph of your son, sir, Colin? Fair haired, blue-eyed, handsome, captain of the school, though not dux. You see sir, in school I was a wimp, a sickly little thing, creeping unwillingly to class. And of course I was bullied, sir. Whipped into the boiler room and set upon in the misty summer mornings and cold winter ones. The leader was tall, blue-eyed, fair-haired. But that was a long time ago. And it is not why I came.

That's sunk forever in the past.
Let us stick unto our last.

HELEN. I'm not sure if I understand what you are saying, Mr Heine. Are you, as I suspect, implying that our son Colin bullied you? That of course is absurd. Colin is now a major in the Education Corps.

HEINE. More congratulations are in order then, Mrs Burnett. How proud you must be.

Sees another photograph.

And this indeed is the relevant photograph with the husband in the peaceful uniform of the Education Corps.

And also here's the blooming bride
of whom the fame is far and wide.

I seem to recall the hair, the lips . . . (*Peers.*)

GEORGE. Her name is Irene, Irene Owens. Her father owns a sports complex.

HEINE. Ah, the fair Irene . . . Indeed, indeed. A lady free and charming. Hospitable.

GEORGE. Sir . . .

HEINE. I am so glad that he is married to the fair Irene. I myself am a bachelor but I do not despise the married state. Indeed I worship it from afar.

Owl.

Listen. What is that?

HELEN. I believe it was an owl.

HEINE. An owl indeed. Nature continues. And also it reminds

me of the lateness of the hour, though you, sir, and you, madam, have been too polite to do so. Tell me, madam, did Colin have a red scar on his fist like the shape of a new moon?

HELEN. He did – but I don't understand why you ask.

HEINE. It is merely the sign of recognition, as in Greek tragedy. But I must come to the nub, I must indeed.

To the nub behoves me come
I hear the beating of the drum.

You see sir, as I have already told you, I am in advertising, an industry awash with money if you have a little talent. And I have my gift for the couplet. And it was you, sir, though you may not remember it, who directed me to that gift, it was indeed. But how can you remember all your pupils. It would not be possible. Some of them perhaps manage factories in sweltering Asia, some may captain ships on the great seas, there is no end to it. Education stretches away in all directions like the ocean. Clear as that mirror, sir, the knowledge of my gift came to me that day.

GEORGE. You must be quick sir, it is late.

HEINE. And we have heard the cry of the owl. Its melancholy tu whit tu whoo, ever nocturnal, ever new. To be brief, sir, you were my teacher for one year.

GEORGE. I must say, sir, I cannot remember. And my wife is getting tired. And so am I. I look at you, sir. I look at you and I can't remember you.

HEINE. Of course you have to eliminate my moustache, sir, and then I am larger now, and then because of your good self I have gained in confidence.

HELEN *gets up.*

GEORGE. Where are you going, dear?

HELEN. I shall go to bed. The hour is late. Good night, Mr Heine, or whoever you are.

HEINE (*rises and bows*). Goodnight, madam.

I hope you have a restful sleep
And no reason for to weep.

She goes and he sits down again.

GEORGE. Now then what is all this, Heine. I have been very patient.

HEINE. Ah how good it is to go to bed with a clear conscience, as you well know, sir, for you have done your best, you have been very diligent and tomorrow you will be honoured before a gathering of your peers.

GEORGE. Who are you, Heine?

HEINE. Yes, I am wasting time. (*More businesslike.*) Let us go back, sir, to a dull morning in the month of November, not an ember of the sun in the sky. I had been given my usual drubbing in the boiler room.

GEORGE. Now look here.

HEINE. I shall not refer to that again, sir.

The boiler room I shall allude
To never again, for it is crude.

So now, Mr Burnett, imagine this classroom whose walls are not well painted, a cockpit for unwilling gladiators. It was dark. And you said to me, Mr Heine, let's have some light on the subject, for I was nearest the switch.

Even in those days you called me Mr Heine.

GEORGE. I cannot . . .

HEINE. Ah but wait sir.

All will come to him who waits
Frivolous or fateful dates.

Anyway you noticed some poems in my jotter. And you asked whose they were and I said mine. But they did not rhyme, sir, and that is the point.

GEORGE. They what?

HEINE. They did not rhyme, sir, You were talking about Pope, sir, that morning and you showed us how good poetry should always rhyme and you took one of my poems, sir, as an example which didn't.

GEORGE. I am quite sure this never . . .

HEINE. Do not distress yourself, sir. In the middle of the laughter and the general barbarism you stood unswerving, sir, though it was as if I had been hit by a bolt of lightning, a vision as it were. Rhyme. That was the answer. Not poems but rhyme. That was the answer. That was what was missing.

GEORGE. Look Heine, or whoever you are, are you trying to make fun of me? Many have tried in the past but I have come down on them like a ton of bricks (*And he brings his hand down on his thigh.*) I have beaten them into submission, sir.

HEINE. Rhyme, sir, that is the secret: not the suffering of the Jew nor his snivelling little self in the boiler room but standing outside himself. Without rhyme, sir, where are we? We are without order. (*Pause.*)

GEORGE. And this is what you came to tell me at this time of night. This . . . rubbish.

HEINE. Ah but sir, you don't seem to understand. You changed my whole life. I went in for advertising. And I have done so well, sir. As a matter of fact I came to offer you a small donation.

He puts his hand in his inside jacket pocket.

GEORGE. Stop there and let me speak. I do not remember you. I don't remember that incident, I think you are making fun of me and, in short, there's the door.

HEINE. I am deeply astounded and disappointed, sir, I came here to contribute to your presentation, I must say, a considerable sum.

HELEN *reappears.*

HELEN. Tell him to go, George.

GEORGE. Don't you hear that . . .

HEINE. Ah well madam, may I say how like a Greek statue you look in your nightgown. Out of a sublime Greek tragedy.

GEORGE. OUT sir.

HEINE. Goodbye sir.

And may your years be true and good
And of a healthy plenitude.

Shalom.

He goes.

GEORGE. Well, who would have believed such ignorance. He must be mad of course. Deranged.

HELEN. Yes.

GEORGE. The cheek. He was going to give me some money. But of course I could not accept it.

HELEN. How strange. And saying how Colin bullied him.

GEORGE. Malicious little Jew.

HELEN. You'd better come to bed.

GEORGE. Yes . . . You know, Helen, I have a very vague . . .

HELEN. Of course you haven't.

GEORGE. No of course not.

HELEN. Quite motiveless as all cranks and evil people are nowadays.

GEORGE. Something about the . . .

HELEN. About the what?

GEORGE. About the . . . humility, the oiliness.

HELEN. Come George.

GEORGE. No, not the humility, the doggishness.

He goes towards her. They look frightened. GEORGE goes to the door and puts out the lights. Darkness descends.

HELEN. Are you there, George?

GEORGE. Yes dear.

HELEN. Good good, you have always been there. A pillar in the dark.

VOICE OF HEINE.
When you go into the dark
Remember the singing of the lark.

End.

A Nick Hern Book

Family first published in Great Britain in 1999 as an original paperback by Nick Hern Books Limited, 14 Larden Road, London W3 7ST, in association with the Traverse Theatre, Edinburgh

One Good Beating was first published in *Scotland Plays*
(Nick Hern Books), 1998. This revised edition first published 1999

Typeset by Country Setting, Kingsdown, Kent CT14 8ES

Printed and bound in Great Britain by Athenaeum Press,
Gateshead NE11 0PZ

A CIP catalogue record for this book is available from
the British Library

ISBN 1 85459 438 9